112 HAIKU

Charleston, SC
www.PalmettoPublishing.com

112 HAIKU
Copyright © 2023 by William Winslow

All rights reserved
No portion of this book may be reproduced, stored in a retrieval system, or transmitted in any form by any means– electronic, mechanical, photocopy, recording, or other– except for brief quotations in printed reviews, without prior permission of the author.

First Edition

Paperback ISBN: 979-8-8229-1735-4

Some of the Haiku here first appeared in an earlier collection of poetry by the author: *Proof I Was Here* (Outskirts Press, 2021).

112
HAIKU

william winslow

DEDICATION

for baggins winnie
lewis sally walker and
sophie – muses all

112 haiku

sturdy hiking stick
carved, sanded, lacquered – oh the
paths we will travel!

crevice in the rock
filled by an early spring rain –
the wood thrush thanks you

leaning into a
brisk autumn wind the moon and
I take the same path

too old to chase deer
he dances before tourists
at the minimart

tiny ant why do you
venture out in such rain –
what is it you seek?

a cheeky squirrel
ate the seed I left out
for a dying red-wing

Beaucatcher tunnel:
once an adventure – now
a short-cut to the malls

airplane view of Silva
and the paper plant – too high
to smell the sulfur

luna moth that light
you are courting will kill you
sooner or later

you will not find it
now – the waterfall has squeezed
back into its rock

a squirrel in the grass -
look, you've left your nose behind
on the window glass!

winter – frozen water
turns its icy back to an
abandoned parkway

william winslow

I've been here before
but these flowers are not like
those of my childhood

inside out outside in —
do you really know which way
you hope to end?

difficult to see
the stars in such rain — have they
washed away for good?

brisk gusts through the groves
leave wind scars on young fruit —
but the sweetness remains

trapped inside this day
by a slow impish rain – she
must have known my plans

old turtle you and
the drainage pipe are one
now that the sun is out

that collar you wear
protects me; you are the free one
but don't seem to care

small frog at the edge
of my newly dug pond – how
far you have traveled!

william winslow

hard rain on the bricks
brings back their colors, removes
all thoughts of the kiln

music for the soul:
dog tags dancing on the rim
of a metal bowl

a paper mill perched
at river's edge – does this card
to you smell as well?

not only do you know
the snail's path but why taken
and how long ago

were you searching for
spring among the tall buildings?
I found only rain

a siren threads the
road below – rousts out the crow
from his nesting place

thanks to a crocus
on this dull blustery day
I am not alone

the old inn at Balsam
perched high above the tracks
where guests disembarked

close by my garden
where I come to rest the road
thrums like a bee swarm

we snore, the dog and I
but when there are complaints
he's my alibi

unable to drive
my father studies road maps
till he falls asleep

tobacco field by
the French Broad – does the wind seem
to catch in your throat?

our walk at first light -
my dog can tell me all the
stories from the night

I have not seen so
small a cricket – what role do
you play in my life?

deer know the length of
my dog's leash and that I'm old
with no desire to run

gutter frog only
now I hear you – did you just
arrive with the rain?

look, the centerpiece
of my garden is that tall
weed I did not plant!

our dog cannot rest
until he knows where we are
and that we are safe

an early sun throws
spiders from the corkscrew
willow against the wall

Sliding Rock your line
is long – before Cherokee
there were the otters

pumpkin leaves reach out
for rain while beneath them
a beetle finds shade

Nagoya to Edo -
moonlight on the rails fast
as the bullet train

an old warrier
with a tin cup and no legs
at Kotokuin Temple

I've not seen the snow
fall in a bamboo grove –
but I hear the silence

ikuradesu ka?
I ask the ivory vendor
on Motomachi

well worth this night climb:
the summit of Mount Fuji
at first sunrise

trimmed, my japanese
yew takes on the look of a
french poodle's tail

feathered bowling pins –
young turkeys stagger among
spent september fields

the year's first falling
leaf against his nose – oh how
my dog rejoices!

not a creek but rain –
we did live by a creek once –
that was long ago

dead limb your tree no
longer needs you – it seems that
we could be brothers

you scatter your bread
too close to the house – yet crows
continue to come

carpenter ants how
busy you are carryng
away my front porch!

tomatoes by the
Broad River – yellow to red
beneath july sun

threat of april rain
makes me hostage to those things
I wish to avoid

my dog ignores the
flowers – seeks only the scent
of a passing deer

I planted this fig
for me – but the birds, squirrels, and
rats think otherwise

a cacophony
of crows at the forest's edge –
a bear passing through

Black Mountain at night
and why not? During the day
it is all color

beauty is brief –
exists only in the colors
of a late autumn

fig tree gnarled by age,
ignored – your fruit is sweeter
with each passing year

a hard rain on the
mountain – only those hungry
come down for our corn

left behind in an
empty house windchimes play songs
of a family lost

what some trees seem to
know about dying could easily
fill a book

an early morning
baptism: bluestem grasses
brush against my legs

encouraged by a
breeze the windchimes tell me just
what they are thinking

silly ant why tug
a leaf so large as that? Wait –
let the wind help you

hot summer rain in
the mountains: heavy and stale -
an old man's breath

william winslow

a rabbit chased off
a crow for our corn – what else
might happen today?

the kidney graphic
a slice of tomato –
life is not so simple

my uncle Cecil
is like a crow: loses a
wife, finds another

overnight wisps of
color waft up through dead leaves –
explode into spring

not yellow brick but
wingstem and aster lead me
through this hillside field

look, a child spattered
mustard along the roadside —
oh, yellow ironweed!

rude rapacious crow,
entitled and fat, you take
my corn for granted

so graceful in death
the falling leaf has no regrets
over beauty lost

brilliant sunset
viewed through a tangle of trees
that filters out the fire

my dog rolls in the
leaves for the smell – I shuffle
through them for the sound

scatterings of my
life on a card table in
the driveway – yard sale

anxious butterfly
in my garden do you see
any sign of spring?

a shed snakeskin in
the backyard – a large one – be
careful where you step!

you are on the phone –
I am undressing you as
I trim the boxwood

azalea in bloom
seems earlier this year –
what else have I missed?

forgotten clothesline
linens pop in the wind – a
restless night ahead!

william winslow

frost warning – cover
our plants the sun is too far
from here to help us!

gentle as soft rain –
let me pass quietly into
the eyes of my dog

obsequious now,
the once vain flower bows to
a late summer rain

no dinner for the
hawk – crows have alerted the
innocent entrée

Roosevelt lies still on
the wet pavement waiting for
me to take him home

now and then Abe, Tom,
and Franklin get together
in my hip pocket

your footprints don't last
in snow so why should I now
think otherwise?

alarmed by my dog
the geese don't know the short
red leash at my side

beneath a blanket
of steel gray sky winter sleeps
heavy in its snow

almost dinner time –
my dog brings me his chew toy
as a reminder

trees give up their leaves
without complaint knowing they
will return in spring

cold slow hands turning
hard soil with a rusted spade –
reaching out for spring

our travels complete
my weary duffle bag sits
alone at the curb

chill winds ripple the
pond – the frog who sang moments
before is silent

blind tiller of soil
drawn by early spring rains –
disrupting my garden

one thing I will not
regret when I pass – that
pile of dirty clothes

william winslow

riding the wind, eyes
sharp as steel needles – not so
easy as it seems

Mount Pisgah – too far
from here to pick berries or
to feel your legs burn

everything but ice
and snow – early spring flowers
curse the almanac

a crystal captures
the july sun – throws rainbows
across my dog's back

bent over and lean –
I have become the tree I
climbed in my childhood!

elf ears scattered on
the forest floor – listening
for winter's approach

that lock of hair I
set aside has not faded –
I had hoped it would

contrails cross but don't
collide in the evening sky
above my garden

my dog moves his sleep
every now and then – it's
the animal in him

deaf – he no longer
spends the day beneath our bed
every first and fourth

spanish moss mirrored
on the pond's still surface – look
at my hair – so long!

hiking stick my hands
have carved you but my legs may
send you on alone

During my two years in Japan I visited numerous shrines, became familiar with Noh and Kabuki theater, rode the bullet train, and climbed Mount Fuji (actually, more of a steep walk). And while I never knowingly encountered Haiku, I did experience and come to appreciate the Japanese minimalist approach to the arts, the importance and symbolism of the seasons, and the Japanese compassion and child-like sense of wonder regarding the world about them.

Most of these Haiku are in what I consider to be the traditional form: 17 syllables (5,7,5), consisting of phrases, fragments, suggestions – in my mind dots which the poet invites the reader to connect and complete the poem.

It has been noted that one characteristic of a Haiku is that it can be said in a single breath. So, set aside some time, take a deep breath, and write yours!

About the Author

William Winslow lives in Mount Pleasant, South Carolina. He earned his BA in English from the Virginia Military Institute, served a tour in Vietnam for which he received a Bronze Star, and later received an MS in Public Administration from the University of Missouri. He is a member of the Poetry Society of South Carolina and has had several competitively selected poems appear in that organization's annual year-book. He is a longtime member of the Academy of American Poets and is a member of the Haiku Society of America.

www.ingramcontent.com/pod-product-compliance
Lightning Source LLC
LaVergne TN
LVHW010442070526
838199LV00066B/6144